GREEN FILES

WILDLIFE IN DANGER

GREEN FILES – WILDLIFE IN DANGER
was produced by

David West ♀♂ Children's Books

7 Princeton Court
55 Felsham Road
London SW15 1AZ

Editor: Gail Bushnell
Picture Research: Carlotta Cooper

First published in Great Britain by Heinemann
Library, Halley Court, Jordan Hill, Oxford
OX2 8EJ, part of Harcourt Education.
Heinemann is a registered trademark
of Harcourt Education Ltd.

07 06 05 04 03
10 9 8 7 6 5 4 3 2 1

ISBN 0 431 18295 7 (HB)
ISBN 0 431 18302 3 (PB)

British Library Cataloguing in Publication Data

Parker, Steve
Wildlife in danger. - (Green Files)
1. Wildlife conservation - Juvenile literature
I. Title
333.9'5416

PHOTO CREDITS :
Abbreviations: t-top, m-middle, b-bottom, r-right,
l-left, c-centre.

Front cover, tl & 29tr (Richard Jones), b & 23b
(SIPA Press) - Rex Features Limited. Pages 4 (Ron
Giling), 5t, 24b (Adrian Arbib), 6t (Peter Weimann),
6–7, 26m (Mark Carwardine), 7bl (Fred Bavenden),
8b (Thomas Raupach), 9t (Julio Etchart), 9b
(Hartmut Schwarzbach), 10b (Ray Pfortner), 10–11
(Daniel Dancer), 11l (Klein/ Hubert) 11tr, 19m, 28m
(Roland Seitre), 11t (Laurent Touzeau), 12b (Aldo
Brando), 14b (J.J. Alcalay), 16t (Lynn Funkhouser),
16br (B&C Alexander), 18t (Anthony Leclerc), 18tr
(Cailey Ermer), 19t (Mark Edwards), 21bm (Pierre
Gleizes), 21br (Tom Walmsley), 22t (Yves Lefevre),
27t (John Maier), 29tl (Michel Gunther), 29b (Cyril
Ruoso), 28bl - Still Pictures. 5b, 6b, 7r, 13b, 17b, 25t
& b, 30 - Corbis Images. 8–9 © Greenpeace/ Grace,
10t Greenpeace/ Rouvillois, 20l © Greenpeace/
Morgan, 20–21 © Greenpeace/ Yashwant, 21t ©
Greenpeace/ Beltra, 21bl © Greenpeace/ Verbelen,
26b © Greenpeace/ Kiryu. 12, 14t - USDA - SCS
Photo. 12–13t © WFP/ FAO Photo. 13t - WFP/ FAO/
F. Betts. 15t (Martin Lee), 15m (Organic Picture
Library), 15b (Wildtrack Media), 16bl (Michael
Dunlea), 19b, 22br (SIPA Press), 22bl (WSPA), 24t
(Andrew Terrill), 29l (Cavendish Press), 28r
(Bachmann), 29r (Per Tormod Nilsen), 3, 4–5, 17t,
18b, 20r, 23t - Rex Features Limited. 26t © WWF/
UK. 28br - Dover Books.

Printed and bound in Italy

*An explanation of difficult words can be
found in the glossary on page 31.*

GREEN FILES

WILDLIFE IN DANGER

Steve Parker

Heinemann
LIBRARY

CONTENTS

Some wildlife adapts to humans, and even thrives. Storks usually nest in high trees, but electricity poles and chimneys do just as well.

All sea turtles are protected by wildlife laws. But it's difficult to enforce these in remote places, especially when people have an age-old tradition of catching turtles for meat, skins and shells.

INTRODUCTION

Many people have a favourite animal, like the fierce and powerful tiger, the strong and silent gorilla, or the cuddly-looking giant panda. But all these are in danger of extinction – dying out completely. Thousands of other creatures face the same threat, from small bugs to giant whales, as well as rare trees, flowers and other plants. The world's natural habitats shrink day by day, under attack from a huge range of human activities. To save wildlife from these dangers is a massive task. Progress is being made – but for some, it could already be too late.

'Eco-tourism', like safaris on African plains, can bring in valuable funds to protect the wildlife on which it is based.

The great apes are gorillas, chimps and orang-utans. They face many dangers from their closest cousins: ourselves.

TRULY WILD?

Some people say that we may be too late to save nature, because there are hardly any truly wild places left. Almost everywhere on our planet has been affected by people.

WHERE'S THE WILDERNESS?

Nearly every 'wilderness' shows signs of human interference. Climbers conquer mountain-tops, rally-drivers cross remote deserts, and polluting chemicals find their way into frozen polar ice-caps and deep oceans. And nowhere can escape the problem of climate change due to global warming.

Gazelles and lions (below) live in nature reserves that aim to recreate a wild environment. Tourists can get close enough to take photographs.

Snow leopards (opposite) live in the world's highest mountains, the Himalayas, but are still killed for fur. Some gorilla troops (left) have full-time guards against poachers.

Hot topic
Antarctica is often called the 'Last Great Wilderness'. But petroleum and mining companies regularly ask for permits to explore. As we run short of fuels and minerals, will we allow the great southern continent to be plundered, spelling disaster for its penguins and other inhabitants?

THE WEB OF NATURE

Animals and plants of all shapes and sizes live together and depend on each other, in an incredibly complex network of relationships called an ecosystem. However when people think about saving wildlife, they usually focus on large or spectacular animals like big cats and eagles. For nature to survive, the whole ecosystem and its habitat must be preserved, not just single species.

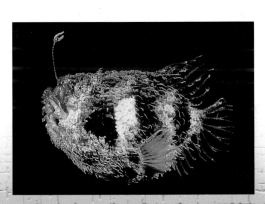

Not long ago, deep-sea anglerfish never saw the light. But now they get hauled up in huge trawl nets. These naturally scarce fish are becoming even rarer.

Emperor penguins, Antarctica.

7

WHO'S MOST DANGEROUS?

The most numerous fairly big creatures on Earth are us – humans. There are more than six billion of us, and our numbers continue to rocket.

PEOPLE AND THEIR ANIMALS

The next most common big animals are on our farms, with some 1,300 million cattle and almost as many sheep. The most numerous fairly big animals which are truly wild, are probably crabeater seals of southern oceans, at 15 million. This astonishing difference shows the dominance of us and our livestock, over the wild creatures of Earth.

Tropical holiday beaches seem inviting and peaceful. But to help reduce risks to bathers, underwater nets take a terrible toll on sharks like the hammerhead – even where attacks are rare.

MORE AND MORE PEOPLE

This graph shows the increasing numbers of people worldwide since 1950, and how the rise is expected to continue. Today, three babies are born every second. The extra people will need land to live and grow their food. So areas available for nature will continue to shrink.

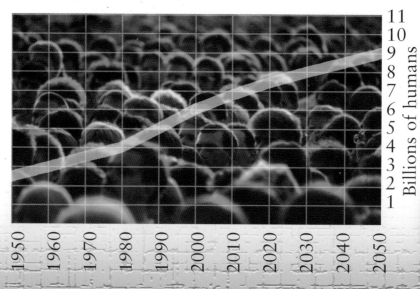

Billions of humans

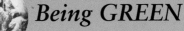

Being GREEN

The 'dash for tourist cash' may greatly alter areas which were once relatively unspoilt. New hotels, roads and visitor centres crowd the land. Traditional ways of life, which were in balance with nature, are being destroyed.

Chitwan, Nepal.

COMFORTABLE LIVES

More than one billion people have comfortable homes and plenty of consumer goods, such as dishwashers, cars and televisions. But this lifestyle damages huge tracts of nature with mines, quarries, oil rigs, cut forests, factories and other industrial needs.

Jetting away on holiday is a welcome break for millions of travellers. But the raw materials and energy needed to build, fuel and operate the plane cause massive environmental damage.

Many different threats face various kinds, or species, of animals and plants. But one danger to the whole of wildlife far outweighs all the rest. This is habitat destruction.

A MULTITUDE OF PROBLEMS

The world's richest wildlife thrives in tropical rainforests – or used to. Enormous areas of rainforest have been cleared, to use the valuable hardwood trees as timber and the land for crops. Rainforests may be the best-known example of habitat loss. Yet many other natural habitats are disappearing daily.

The world's forests are being destroyed at a dramatic rate, yet they are especially valuable. They could yield vital substances like new medicines.

Wetlands may look dull and empty. But their natural value is huge, as nursery areas for baby fish and other water creatures, and stop-overs for migrating birds.

Hot topic

The golden lion tamarin is a small monkey of rainforests in Brazil. It was nearly wiped out by the 1970s, as its forests were logged and cleared. But the plight of this attractive creature led to great public outcry. In the 1990s its numbers rose again – along with other animals of its habitat.

A golden lion tamarin.

The only major habitat which is increasing in size is the urban one. And only a few 'pest' species benefit from it, like red foxes, brown rats, house mice and cockroaches.

SOMEWHERE TO LIVE

We can aim to save 'symbols of conservation' like tigers and gorillas, in a few nature parks or reserves. But if their original homes are disappearing too, along with the animals and plants which play such important roles in their lives, eventually they will have nowhere to live wild. Our efforts are wasted.

RAINFORESTS IN DANGER

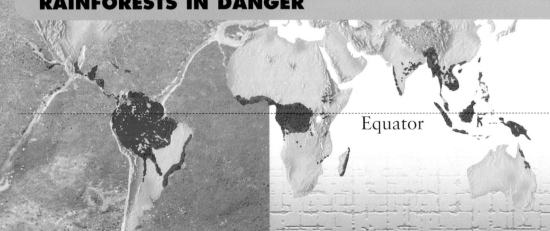

Equator

More than half of the original rainforests were destroyed in the past century. The remainder, shown in dark green, are still being removed at a terrifying rate, with the major 'hot-spots' of destruction in red.

11

One type of 'wild'-erness is a place unaffected by humans, where animals and plants still live as they did in ancient times. But 'wilderness' can also mean a place with limited biodiversity, meaning a decline in the varieties and numbers of living things.

In the 1930s, over-farming and dry conditions made areas of the USA into 'dust bowls' (background). This nation was rich enough to recover, unlike many countries today.

MONOCULTURE

Many such 'wildernesses' are farmlands or planted forests. One crop, such as wheat or pine trees, stretches farther than the eye can see. Almost no other plants, and hardly any animals, survive in this monoculture or 'one growth'.

Hot topic

Even creatures on the ocean floor are not safe from hunters. Divers collect them in nets, but the biggest threats are the huge fishing boats that drag massive trawls and other nets through the sea, scraping up all forms of life. As the nets are hauled in, many creatures are unwanted and thrown back – dead.

Shellfish are at risk from divers too.

DESERTIFICATION

The most common form of habitat degradation is desertification. Farm animals overgraze, or eat away grasses and other plants almost entirely. The plant roots die, and no longer hold moisture in the soil or keep the particles together. In the dry season the upper layers of soil are easily blown away – or a rare rainstorm washes it away.

As people try to survive at the desert's edge, their cattle, sheep, goats and camels graze and trample the soil. It loses its nutrient goodness and the animals starve.

1 Plant roots bind soil together.

2 Overgrazing kills off roots, allowing loose soil to dry, crumble and blow away.

LIVING ON THE EDGE

Every year the world's biggest desert grows larger. The Sahara's southern edge creeps south by 3–5 kilometres. People living in these dry, scrubby lands try to grow crops and raise livestock. But the soil is thin and poor, and droughts are regular. The soil turns to dusty sand, adding to the Sahara. The same process, known as habitat degradation, is happening in many other places.

Conifer trees are poor for wildlife, yet more and more of these fast-growing trees are being planted, to provide much of the world's softwood timber.

Grasslands grow where the climate is too dry for woods and forests, but too moist for scrub and desert. The problem is that 'unnatural' grasslands are spreading and thriving worldwide. These grasslands are planted with farm crops and only support a small variety of wildlife.

Natural grasslands include North American prairies, South American pampas, African savannahs and Asian steppes. Their plentiful, natural grasses and plants support some spectacular animals, like the American bison. Now most are farmed and their wildlife has gone.

CEREAL CROPS

'Unnatural' grasslands are those planted with a crop like wheat, barley, rye, maize, rice, oats, sorghum and millet. These are all cereal or 'grain' plants, and members of the grass family.

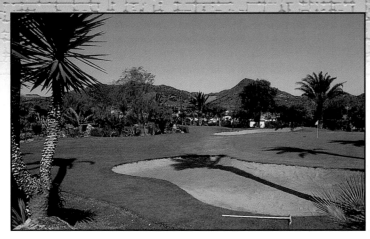

Grasses thrive on a small scale on lawns, parks and golf courses. But most of these are mowed and weeded, to keep natural variety at bay.

Hot topic

Modern 'intensive' farming uses machines and pesticides and other chemicals. Organic farms reject such methods, avoiding chemical pollutants and nurturing the soil with natural fertilizers that allows a greater variety of life.

PAMPERED GRASS

Cereal crops cover three-quarters of the world's farmland. Farmers look after these vast monocultures (see page 12) carefully, feeding the land with fertilizers. Herbicides are used against weeds and pesticides kill insects, so very little wildlife is able to survive.

Native grasses such as kangaroo-grass and spinifex once thrived in the Australian outback. Ranchers have sown great areas with other grasses, more suitable for grazing livestock.

Organic farm, England.

15

Long ago, people were hunter-gatherers. They obtained all their food from the wild, by hunting animals for meat and gathering plant parts like fruits, nuts and berries.

TRADITIONAL WAYS

A few people still follow these traditional ways, like Inuit in the far north and Aboriginals in Australia. But elsewhere, using modern technology, foods are taken from the wild on a huge scale. African bushmeat, for example, is a growing trade and is sold throughout the world.

A deadly trend in tropical areas is dynamite-fishing. Whole reefs are blasted, killing many fish.

In Arctic regions, Inuit people have hunted seals for thousands of years, taking only the seals they need and using almost all body parts for clothes and food. In Africa, rare species, including antelopes, gorillas and wild pigs are killed and traded, and much is discarded.

Being GREEN

Vast curtain-like drift nets are set to catch tuna and similar fish. But dolphins like tuna too, get trapped and drown. Such accidental deaths can be avoided using 'dolphin-friendly' net designs.

Dolphin-unfriendly.

EXPLOITED TO DEATH

Fast boats with harpoons almost wiped out great whales. They were protected in the 1980s. The same over-exploitation is happening now to other sea animals, from dolphins to turtles.

DISAPPEARING FISH

Year after year, fishing fleets struggle to find more fish to catch. Because they have been so successful in the past, many places are now 'fished out'. In areas like the North Sea, the numbers of fish such as cod have collapsed.

Commercial fishing nets all kinds of animals, not just 'target' species. Between one-tenth and one-third of the catch is 'non-target' but still injured or killed. This includes young fish who cannot then grow up to breed.

North-east Atlantic
11m

North-east
Pacific
2.5m

North-west
Atlantic
2.5m

Mediterranean
and Black Sea
1.7m

North-west
Pacific
30m

West-central
Atlantic
2m

East-central
Atlantic
2m

West Indian
4.1

West-central
Pacific
10m

South-
west
Pacific
1m

East-
central
Pacific
5m

South-east
Atlantic
1m

East Indian
4m

South-west
Atlantic
2.5m

Antarctic
Indian Ocean
0.1m

Antarctic
Atlantic
0.3m

South-east Pacific
12m

Numbers show millions of tonnes of fish and other sea animals caught each year.

17

UNNATURAL ENEMIES

A rabbit nibbles grass, but suddenly dashes away as a red fox comes near. It seems like an age-old scene from nature – but not in Australia.

SPREADING AROUND

The island continent of Australia has suffered more than most places from the ravages of introduced or alien species. These are animals and plants which have been taken from their natural or native homes, to new areas. The introductions are usually carried out by people, deliberately or accidentally.

The red squirrel was common in English mixed woodland. From about 1900 its US grey cousin was introduced and began to take over at the expense of the red squirrels.

UNWANTED VISITORS

Animals and plants have always spread to new regions, by natural means such as seeds in the wind, or creatures carried on a tree drifting out to sea. But people have speeded up the process thousands of times. Some of our introductions are deliberate, like goats as hardy farm animals. Others are 'stowaways' like brown rats and house mice.

Rabbits went to Australia with the first European colonists. By the 1880s they had spread and destroyed vast areas of plant life.

Birds easily fly to new lands.

Plant seeds arrive in bird droppings.

Insects and seeds blow on the wind.

Plants and animals drift on ocean currents.

Humans arrive with pets and pests.

One of the most widespread invaders, hiding away on cargo ships, is the brown rat. It eats many foods, including eggs. In New Zealand it is a major threat to the rare, flightless, ground-nesting bird, the takahe. Rats eat its eggs. Saving the takahe would mean exterminating these pests.

Takahe bird, New Zealand.

Goats are useful farm animals who can survive on tough vegetation. But this makes them very destructive, especially where local plants have no thorns or poisons to deter them.

OUT OF BALANCE

In its native home, a species is usually kept in check by predators, harsh weather or disease. In a new environment, these natural checks could be absent. The species can multiply rapidly, upset the local ecology and even cause its new neighbours to become extinct.

Water hyacinths spread from tropical America and now choke many waterways worldwide.

19

Pollution and waste affect big cities, with smog in the air, dirt in the rivers and litter on the streets. But toxins and other pollutants spread, harming wildlife.

GLOBAL DANGERS

Harmful chemicals like PCBs (polychlorinated biphenyls) are used in plastics and electrical equipment. They are released by dumping or burning, then they spread into the environment quickly, but break down slowly. These chemicals have been detected in the remotest lands. They have even been found inside polar bears!

Many countries have laws to stop polluting chemicals in rivers and lakes. 'Accidents' like this spill from an Indian factory may be deliberate.

Highly visible pollution of oil slicks kills marine life like fish and birds. But invisible chemicals take a greater toll.

Hot topic

Some campaign groups use direct action and even risk injury to gain publicity. Their aim is to make people more aware of the dangers to wildlife and our shared environment. These activists are reducing the flow from a chemical factory waste pipe in north-east England.

Greenpeace take action.

Dead fish litter the bank after toxic sludge escapes into a river in Spain (inset). Rivers carry pollution hundreds of kilometres and out to sea.

ALONG THE FOOD CHAINS

As polluting chemicals spread through air, soil and water, they are a special danger to larger predatory animals like birds of prey, big cats and sharks. Pollutants are taken at low levels into plants. Herbivores eat these and take in more. Predators consume the herbivores, and levels rise still higher (below).

BIO-AMPLIFICATION

Pesticide sprays get into crops (1). Small animals like mice (2) eat these and gather the chemicals in their bodies. The same happens as the owl (3) eats the mice. The way that toxins become more concentrated along a food chain to harm top predators is called bio-amplification.

In richer nations, chemicals are gradually improved to lessen pollution. But older versions are sold to other countries and used without proper protection.

Beluga (white whales) have been found with high levels of toxins in their bodies. Demonstrators raise public awareness to the dumping of toxic waste in oceans (inset).

Some kinds of animals face a special threat: poaching. This is when creatures are caught or killed against the law. There are ways to tackle poaching, but some governments try to ignore it.

WHY ANIMALS ARE POACHED

Some animals are captured alive, usually for the exotic pet trade. Colourful birds like parrots and macaws, monkeys and apes such as baby chimps and orang-utans, snakes, fish and even spiders are at risk. Other creatures are killed for body parts like fur coats, ivory tusks of elephants and walruses, horns, antlers, teeth, bones, even blood and body fluids.

Being GREEN
Some pet shops deal in exotic fish species, like seadragons, and tropical birds. They should have clear notices about getting their animals from captive breeding sources, rather than trapping in the wild. Anyone who is suspicious of pet shops or suppliers is encouraged to contact the local authorities.

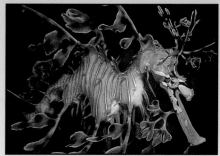

Seadragons are threatened.

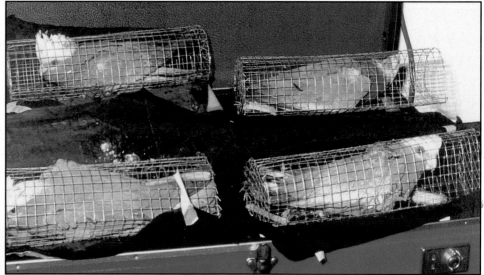

Some poachers specialize in stealing babies to be brought up by humans as pets – then probably abandoned.

Live animals, like these Galah birds, are smuggled in terrible conditions. The animals often die in pain.

A magnificent rhino slaughtered for its horn.

SUPPLY AND DEMAND

Rare or valuable animals can be protected by guards and rangers. A long-term solution is to remove the demand. Perhaps people could do without gorilla-hand ashtrays or rhino-horn knife handles and be taught that powdered tiger-bone 'medicine' has no healing value. The world agreement against poaching is the Convention on International Trade in Endangered Species, CITES.

Some African countries show their support of an ivory trade ban by burning elephant tusks, which have been seized from poachers.

23

Around the world, thousands of wildlife parks, reserves, refuges and sanctuaries have been set up to protect animals and plants. But only some are successful.

LOCAL NEEDS

Many threatened species and habitats are in poor regions, where people struggle to survive. They may resent the land set aside for animals and the money spent on rangers and visitor centres, while their families go hungry. If local people are involved in running parks and using the income, there is greater chance of success.

Hot topic

Plants, as well as animals, are in danger of being taken from the wild, to sell to collectors. 'Cactus-rustling' is big business in parts of the Americas. It's difficult to patrol the huge areas of dry scrub and protect these rare and beautiful plants, which may flower only once every 100 years.

Cacti bloom in Mexico.

Tourists shop and drink at an African nature park – but who benefits from their money?

SAVE THE TIGER - AND OTHERS TOO

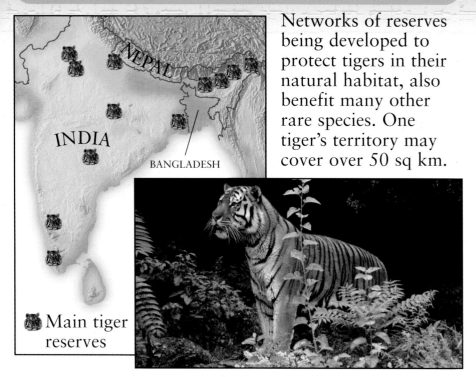

Networks of reserves being developed to protect tigers in their natural habitat, also benefit many other rare species. One tiger's territory may cover over 50 sq km.

INDIA

NEPAL

BANGLADESH

Main tiger reserves

Tigers need their own territories.

BIGGER IS BETTER

Big predators like tigers and eagles need huge territories to roam and hunt, and greater areas to search for mates. If they are crammed into small reserves they may mate with related individuals and suffer from problems of genetic inbreeding. Some reserves are linked by 'corridors' or pathways for use when mating, to find unrelated partners.

FAILING TO SAVE THE FISH

Fishing alters the balance of nature in coastal lagoons, even affecting birds like greater flamingoes.

Banc d'Arguin is Africa's largest marine sanctuary, stretching hundreds of kilometres along the west coast. It was set up in 1976 to protect breeding areas for mullet and other fish. But giant trawlers now patrol its borders and catch fish coming to breed.

Banc d'Arguin National Park

AFRICA

ATLANTIC OCEAN

Famous threatened species like gorillas and pandas will only survive if we save their whole habitats. But such 'headline' species also bring valuable publicity.

FOCUS ON THE FAMOUS

'Headline' species are usually big, spectacular, fierce, cuddly – or all of these. They grab the news and feature in campaigns, at the expense of thousands of other threatened species. Often, however, they help to raise general awareness about saving wildlife.

Being GREEN

'Adopt an animal' schemes help to get people personally involved with wildlife conservation. The adopters can follow news of their animal and, if local, visit it. Whole schools, streets and commercial companies can also adopt, or sponsor a species.

WWF adoption form for a rhino.

Mass slaughter of great whales like the blue was mostly stopped in the 1980s. However many of their smaller cousins are still not protected and are still being killed.

In recent years only one male Spix macaw has survived in the wild, in north-east Brazil. There are over 50 in captivity. Saving the species depends entirely on breeding them.

All five rhino species need our protection. Four are faced with dying out. The Sumatran rhino is the smallest and hairiest rhino – and just a couple of hundred remain.

GOING, GOING ... GONE!

For some kinds of animals and plants, conservation comes too late. It's estimated that there could be over 20 million species of living things in the world, and one becomes extinct every few hours. Most of these are bugs and similar small animals in remote places like dense rainforests. They took millions of years to evolve, yet they are wiped out quickly.

When European settlers arrived in North America, vast flocks of passenger pigeons darkened the skies. Shooting, trapping and poisoning killed off the whole species by 1914.

In 1938, a law was introduced to protect the Australian thylacine, or 'Tasmanian tiger'. It was too late. The last known one died in 1933.

Some people do not like to see animals in captivity, held in pens or behind fences. But for some species there is no other option, apart from dying out completely.

IMPORTANT KNOWLEDGE

Animals in captivity cannot live exactly as they would in nature. But they can be studied by zoologists and other scientists. This builds up vital knowledge about what the animals eat, how they breed, and other information to help save them in the wild.

During the 1980s the number of Californian condors fell to about 20. All were captured for breeding – a decision that caused huge argument at the time. Today there are over 160, with about 50 released to the wild.

About 1,000 giant pandas are left in the wild, in south-west China. Efforts to breed them in city zoos had mixed results. Research centres set up in their habitats are more successful.

Captive breeding saved the Arabian oryx, a rare kind of antelope. It was extinct in the wild by 1972. Small herds from wildlife parks were released from 1982, and now thrive.

Hot topic

Killer whale Keiko was star of the *Free Willy* movies. But when Keiko was himself released, after 22 years in captivity, he preferred to stay near people rather than swim away. He lives in a bay in Norway with his human 'friends', now free to go whenever he wishes.

Keiko: *human company.*

PLACES TO LIVE

Captive breeding has helped to save dozens of species from disaster. But there are problems. If the original threat to an animal was habitat loss or poaching, will there be anywhere safe to release captive-bred individuals? Some creatures like whales, elephants and apes need long periods of learning when young – what to eat, which predators to avoid, and where to travel in their habitat. This is difficult to provide in captivity.

Baby apes like orang-utans rely on their mothers to teach them survival skills, such as which fruits to eat.

Animals and plants are worth saving for so many reasons: pleasure, beauty, excitement, fascination, scientific knowledge, and possible new products like medicines from rainforests.

STILL IN DANGER

However it's difficult for us to decide which species should be saved. We need to think about saving nature as a whole complex system. Why not start an initiative in your school to support a species at a local zoo? You could learn more about their habitat and the dangers that face them in the wild.

Addresses and websites for further information

WWF
Panda House,
Weyside Park,
Godalming,
Surrey,
GU7 1XR
Tel 01483 426444
www.panda.org
WWF (formerly WorldWide Fund For Nature) leads international efforts to conserve nature and protect the diversity of life on Earth.

WWF AUSTRALIA
PO Box 528,
Sydney,
NSW 2001
Tel 02 9281 5515
Fax 02 9281 1060
www.wwf.net.au

Greenpeace UK
Canonbury Villas,
London,
N1 2PN
Tel 020 7865 8100
Fax 020 7865 8200
E-mail
info@uk.greenpeace.org
www.greenpeace.org.uk
Powerful campaigning organization, supporting taking action against those who damage wildlife and sites of natural beauty.

THE WILDLIFE TRUSTS (UK)
The Kiln,
Waterside,
Mather Road,
Newark,
Nottinghamshire,
NG24 1WT
Tel 0870 0367711
www.wildlifetrusts.org/
The Wildlife Trusts partnership is dedicated to wildlife and conservation.

IUCN
International Union for the Conservation of Nature and Natural Resources.
www.iucn-uk.org
Tel 01733 866844
The World Conservation Union who monitor wildlife worldwide, and help to save threatened species.

FRIENDS OF THE EARTH
26-28 Underwood Street,
London,
N1 7JQ
Tel 020 7490 1555
Fax 020 7490 0881
www.foe.co.uk
The largest international network of environmental groups, campaigning for the conservation of species and wild places.

GLOSSARY

adapted
Having skills or features which help an animal, plant or person to survive in a particular place, such as the thick fur of the polar bear, which keeps it warm in the Arctic.

biodiversity
A measure of the number of different kinds of living things in a particular place.

ecology
The scientific study of how a community of plants and animals live together in their surroundings.

ecosystem
A community of plants and animals in their physical environment, and especially how they live together and interact with each other.

extinct
When a certain kind or species of living thing dies out completely, so there are none left anywhere in the world, and the species cannot be brought back.

environment
The surroundings including soil, rocks, water, air, plants, animals and even man-made structures.

habitat
A particular type of environment or surroundings, with certain kinds of plants and animals, such as a river, grassland, desert or rainforest.

herbicide
A chemical substance designed to kill plants. Most especially target weeds, leaving crops unharmed.

pesticide
A substance designed to kill or disable pests such as insects, mainly on farm crops or animals.

pollutant
A substance that causes harm or damage to our surroundings, including wildlife and ourselves.

predators
Animals that hunt and feed on other animals.